Reading-
A Novel Approach

Written by **Janice Szabos**

Illustrated by **Vanessa Filkins**

Cover by Vanessa Filkins
Copyright © Good Apple, Inc., 1984
ISBN No. 0-86653-186-6

Good Apple
A Division of Frank Schaffer Publications, Inc.
23740 Hawthorne Boulevard
Torrance, CA 90505-5927

TABLE OF CONTENTS

INTRODUCTION

Reading—A Novel Approach presents an instructional program for the use of novels in the classroom. The program is designed to enrich the reading experiences of children in grades four through eight. The novel is seen as a vehicle for explorations which involve critical and creative thinking. Students become actively involved in every phase of the program and are guided toward a better understanding of the thinking processes.

The program revolves around student discussion groups during which they learn to listen and to share points of view, ideas, and feelings.

A wide variety of student activities permits the teacher and students to approach each reading section flexibly. These activity sheets are coded according to Bloom's level of cognitive thinking.

Each activity is reproducible and can be used with the novel approach or any other reading program. The discussion group training and record-keeping system can be used with basal readers and other reading programs.

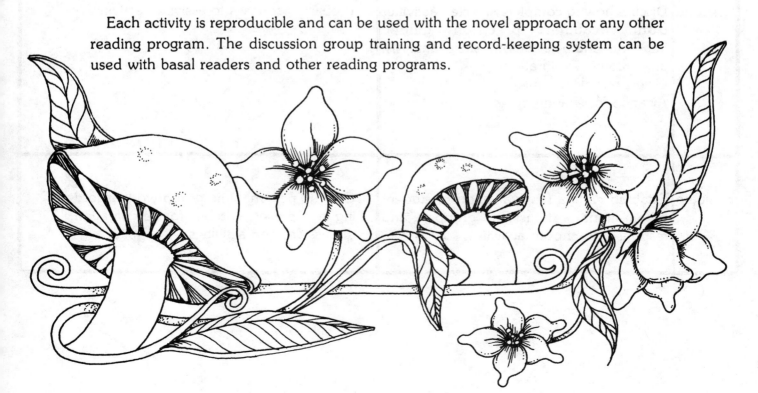

THE NOVEL APPROACH ORGANIZATIONAL FRAMEWORK

	Teacher	Students
Prepare	Select novel. Read. Form discussion questions. Form student groups. Teach Bloom's Taxonomy (optional). Train group in discussion skills. Prepare schedule. Assign readings, questions, activities. Explain record keeping.	Read assigned sections. Develop working knowledge of Bloom's Taxonomy. Learn good discussion skills. Prepare responses to questions and activities. Keep records up to date.
Discuss the Novel	Facilitate discussion groups. Observe, encourage. Solve problems when necessary.	Be prepared. Interact with discussion group. Share thoughts, feelings, and ideas. Help others to share. Accept leadership of group when asked.
Respond	Discuss how to complete selected activities from vocabulary precision, guided imagery, characterization, story analysis, and creative explorations. Give examples as needed. Arrange for sharing times.	Prepare responses to assigned activities.
Evaluate	Establish criteria for evaluation of student preparations, discussion groups, and responses to chosen activities.	Critique personal and group work according to preset criteria for preparation, discussion, and activities.

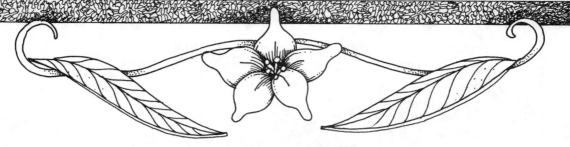

THE NOVEL APPROACH

By looking beyond basal reading texts and standard literature anthologies, teachers, especially those responsible for enrichment classes, can help students explore the wonderful variety of novels available as trade books. Selections in paperback form can be made to meet the particular needs and interests of varied groups of students and can be chosen to blend specifically with a particular theme or area of study. Challenging work can be presented in one classroom at a variety of reading levels by forming several groups at different levels, with each group reading a different novel related to the same theme.

In identifying material for enrichment, there is a special need to use challenging works which will present students with new demands for thoughtful analysis and judgment. Popular works are not necessarily the best. Short selections do not allow for extended analysis and discovery of patterns, themes and interrelationships available in novels.

Many students are ready to reach far beyond the standard decoding and comprehension skills. The program for these learners should help them to develop critical and creative thinking skills applicable to real-life problems.

To Be a Better Reader:

visualize more creatively
think more deeply
analyze your thinking
share and evaluate your thoughts with others

To Be a Better Reading Teacher:

get your students involved in all of the above!

The program and activities presented in *Reading—A Novel Approach* were designed with this goal in mind.

Teacher Preparation

NOVEL SELECTION

Choosing the correct novel for a particular group is the teacher's first task. Aside from the desire to locate a novel related to a particular time period, location, theme, or interest, two major considerations exist.

The novel selected should offer the student a special richness of language, complexity of theme, and variance of style so that the reader is forced to think about what is being presented both at a surface level and in a more symbolic sense. A wide use of figures of speech should be present. Analogies should be abundant and thought provoking. The plot should be complex and unique. The story may present a paradox, the ending may be nonexistent, or the setting may be rich in fantasy and timelessness.

The second consideration in novel selection should be the readability level of the book and the maturity level of the students. It is sometimes difficult to match the two and find material that remains within the realm of the child's maturity and yet offers sufficient challenge to an advanced reading level. Good professional judgment is essential.

FORMING QUESTIONS

The formation of suitable questions can be fairly easy if the questioner will keep in mind their basic purpose: to stimulate analytical discussion. Good questions should demand responses which encompass a problem, issue, or time reference, trace a feeling or pattern of action, or show a trend over an entire section of the book. Questions should be at the analysis level in which the learner is asked to identify several passages from the reading which will allow the reader to compare, contrast, dissect, categorize, take apart, or in some way show a deep understanding well beyond finding the "correct" recall-type answer.

Samples:

1. Cite several passages to show Jim's feelings about the journey.

2. Which character showed the most aggression in this section? What do you feel caused it?

3. What were people's attitudes toward the stranger? How did they justify their actions and feelings?

4. They say "Beauty is in the eye of the beholder." How does this apply to the section you have just read?

5. In what way do you see Meg's actions as being "out of character" for her?

USE OF BLOOM'S TAXONOMY

Perhaps the most important reading tools for enrichment would be skills to develop critical thinking. Benjamin Bloom's *Taxonomy of Educational Objectives* has been selected as a functional cognitive outline for use by teachers and students in understanding the varying levels of cognitive thought with the goal of developing the higher levels—analysis, synthesis, and evaluation.

One section of this work presents students with training activities in using Bloom's Taxonomy. These activities are an optional part of the novel approach and as such would be included as preparatory work before beginning the novel cycle.

THE DISCUSSION CIRCLE

The center of success in using the novel approach with students is the discussion circle, a weekly gathering of the small group of students. This sharing of ideas and images, guided by teacher-chosen discussion questions, enhances each individual's perception of events and characters up to that point in the novel.

The discussion circle is student directed and evaluated. The teacher observes the interaction and serves as a facilitator as needed.

Students are encouraged to share their responses to the week's questions and their general thoughts and feelings about the novel in an informal manner. Leadership of the group should be assumed by each member on a rotating basis. The leader encourages all members to contribute, keeps the discussion moving, and guides the group evaluation of the discussion period.

Students learn to accept the opinions of others and practice the fine art of courteous disagreement as well as the skill of listening to others' comments to add more details or information without repetition.

At all times members may request the citation (page, paragraph) from the book to clarify an answer or an interpretation.

Skill-Developing Activities

To develop in the reader the ability to go beyond the printed word, to interpret ideas presented in the theme of the novel, and to make new connections, we must expand our skills expectations both in content and depth.

Reading—A Novel Approach offers extension activities in five areas: Guided Imagery, Characterization, Vocabulary Precision, Story Analysis, and Creative Explorations. Each reproducible activity sheet is coded to the levels of Bloom's Taxonomy by letters in the upper left-hand corner.

Teachers should select appropriate skill-developing activities for each week's work and spend some time discussing expected responses with the students. The teacher's Six Week Plan sheet (see page 17) allows space for recording those activities you choose.

It is suggested that sharing of responses to skill activities be done in the small group on a day separate from the novel discussion day to allow adequate preparation time and suitable time for sharing.

Guided Imagery

For reading to be meaningful, the reader selects from a personal background of experiences those images which seem to relate to the printed word. The more rich and varied the images, the more intense will be those relationships. Image making occurs not only from direct experiences but also from the mind's world of fantasy. Concepts and theory must first be part of the mind's image-imagination! Critical thinking can become a more conscious process as we develop in students the ability to understand and use their minds. Recent research on the brain and learning implications of these studies suggests the importance of helping students use visual imagery as a learning tool.

The specialized techniques of helping students take imaginary trips in their minds are presented in several books:

Eberle, Bob. *Scamper: Games for Imagination Development*. Buffalo, New York: D.O.K. Publishers, 1971.

Harrison, A., and Diann Musical. *Other Ways, Other Means*. Santa Monica, California: Goodyear, 1978.

Hendricks, Gay and Russell Wills. *The Centering Book*. Englewood Cliffs, New Jersey: Prentice Hall, 1975.

Plum, Lorraine. *Flights of Fantasy*. Carthage, Illinois: Good Apple, Inc., 1980.

Wayman, Joe and Lorraine Plum. *Secrets and Surprises*. Carthage, Illinois: Good Apple, Inc., 1977.

If you choose to explore this area on your own, just remember your purpose is to help students expand their thinking in a more visual, imaginative way (right-brain activities). To this end it is important to encourage student relaxation of body and then concentration on mental pictures and sensory impressions. Reading descriptive passages in which students become part of the experience is helpful.

Another type of reading selection is one in which students are encouraged to take a simple object like a chair and make it change magically in their minds (smaller, larger, embellished, as a vehicle, different colors, designs, types, etc.)

Writing a mind journey is challenging and fun both for students and teachers. Imagery experiences should be presented to students as *serious* whimsical business for mind development!

Characterization

The skill section on characterization helps students identify the subtleties of personality presented by the author. Students are asked to analyze personal thoughts and feelings as they see themselves reflected in characters and events in the novel.

Vocabulary Precision

Activities in Vocabulary Precision encourage students to look upon activities as a personal challenge. The students' natural love for words is used as a vehicle for helping them identify, analyze, and create new uses for vocabulary learning.

Story Analysis

In the Story Analysis section, students are asked to explore the story sequence, the plot, setting, style and theme. Many activities provide experiences with complex analysis. Problem-solving techniques are discussed and a deliberate attempt has been made to help students visualize story components through webs, diagrams, charts, and shape outlines.

Creative Explorations

The creative explorations are intended for frequent use as idea expanders. The activities help students use their special thinking skills and creative talents in unique ways. They are mind expanders which stress fluency, flexibility, originality, and elaboration.

To the Teacher: Evaluation

While teacher evaluations of students are very personal, the novel approach does present great expectations for student involvement in the evaluative process. Final grades should certainly take these student evaluations into account, and personal evaluations completed by students should weigh heavily in judging progress toward developing critical thinking skills.

Learning activities will become more meaningful as students select their own standards and objectives. The creation of personal and group evaluative instruments should be encouraged. Sample forms for evaluation are included in the Forms section, pages 16-23.

RECORD KEEPING

The Forms section includes outline sheets for both students and teachers. It is important for students to develop a regular system for maintaining records of their responses to novel questions and skill activities. They will often want to refer back to some previous work or discussion. For this reason it is suggested that they organize and maintain novel notebooks or spirals as discussed in the Student Preparation section, pages 12-15.

Teachers are also encouraged to keep notebooks for the novels which include not only their assigned questions and time plans, but also good student examples of work and discussion points which will serve as a valuable resource when using the same novel with another group in the future.

To the Teacher: Getting Them Started

Once you have chosen the novel, formed questions, and prepared your work outline sheet for the entire novel, the final preparatory task for the teacher involves planning activities for helping students get started.

A general overview of the novel approach should be presented to the group. This could be an entire class activity if all students will be using the novel approach at the same time.

Student papers (for Getting Started page 13, Student Preparation Check Sheet page 19, and Discussion Responsibilities page 14) should be distributed and discussed.

A sample reading selection (about 15-20 pages in length) and a sample question should be presented and completed as a group to help clarify procedures. The Student Record form and Question Responses sheets should be used.

A mock discussion should be held with the teacher becoming a member of the group (serving in the Leader's role). Clarify procedures and work to define and refine discussion techniques.

Help students evaluate group discussion work and prepare sample personal evaluations.

Since Planned Experience Activities vary greatly, each should be discussed separately as it is assigned.

The novel approach as outlined on the teacher's Six Week Plan sheet can then be divided into weekly cycles. A suggested time schedule would be:

Day one	-	Assign section reading and questions from the novel.
Day two	-	Have reading discussion groups.
Day three	-	Summarize reading and choose skill-developing activities.
Day four	-	Prepare skill activities.
Day five	-	Discuss and share skill activities.

To the Student: Getting Started

The novel study is designed to help you get more out of your reading and share your experiences with others. This study is different from pleasure reading in that your reading is programmed by sections for study, discussion, and activity.

Since many of your activities are done in a small group, your responsibilities go beyond personal ones. The others will depend on you to do your best and be prepared.

A loose-leaf notebook divided into the following sections will help you to organize your work:

1. Student Responsibilities
2. Evaluation Sheets
3. Novel Question Activity Records
4. Bloom's Taxonomy
5. Guided Images
6. Characterization
7. Story Analysis
8. Vocabulary Precision
9. Creative Explorations

Each week's work can be placed in the appropriate section.

Your teacher will present you with these questions for each week's reading section. These are really meant more for guiding your reading and group discussion than for the merits of a specific answer.

Write the question on a Student Record form. This form also has space for recording activities (planned experiences) assigned by your teacher or selected for that week by you.

Answer the questions on the Question Responses form. Whenever you find a place in the novel that would help you explain your direct answer to one of the questions, record page number, paragraph (first, second, etc.), key words (the first two words of the paragraph), and a *brief* comment that will remind you of what you want to say in response to that particular question. You *never* answer the questions in sentence form. You *do* find *several* places in the novel for each question's answer. There is no one correct place to find the answer.

As you read your novel section, underline new or interesting vocabulary words. Each week's activities will include some vocabulary work.

Your teacher will select or help you choose several experience activities to complete your requirements for the week's work.

DISCUSSION RESPONSIBILITIES

Leader

1. Briefly review the novel to date.

2. Read questions for discussion in turn.

3. Encourage courteous interaction of members.

4. Summarize group's response to each question.

5. Guide group evaluation of discussion period.

6. Select next week's leader.

7. Present brief report to teacher. Include members absent or unprepared, general quality of discussion, name of next week's leader.

Group Members

1. Be prepared for discussion.

2. Back up statements with evidence from reading.

3. Listen attentively.

4. Add to idea presented or indicate agreement or courteous disagreement.

5. Respect the opinions of others.

6. Speak only one at a time.

7. Participate in a fair evaluation of the group's work.

To the Student: Evaluation

At the conclusion of each week's work, it is important for you to help assess your group's discussion work and your contributions. You should also make some judgment about the quality of the other planned experiences you complete.

The Discussion Evaluation sheet should also be completed at the conclusion of a section of work. These Personal Evaluation sheets may be revised to better suit your needs, or replaced completely by journal/log type entries where you would record your thoughts and feelings about activities you complete.

The evaluation process allows you to become fully involved in deciding whether or not you have successfully met the criteria or have been able to identify strong and weak areas.

Discussion
Evaluation Sheet

Six-Week Plan

Novel _____

Week	Questions		Vocabulary Precision	Guided Imagery	Characterization	Story Analysis	Creative Explorations
I pages							
II pages							
III pages							
IV pages							
V pages							
VI pages							

TEACHER PREPARATION CHECK SHEET

_____ 1. Select appropriate novel

_____ 2. Read novel. Underline suitable vocabulary words.

_____ 3. Divide a novel into 6-8 uniform sections. Each section will represent a week's work.

_____ 4. Develop three analysis questions for each section.

_____ 5. Prepare work outline sheet for entire novel, selecting appropriate activities.

_____ 6. Form student groups (5-8 members).

_____ 7. Select evaluation procedures.

Notes

_____

_____

_____

_____

_____

_____

_____

_____

_____

STUDENT PREPARATION CHECK SHEET

_____ Read selection for pleasure. Then reread.

_____ Identify and underline new or interesting words.

_____ Read to record responses to questions.

_____ Think about how events in this section relate to the novel as a whole.

_____ Be prepared to discuss events and any hidden or deeper meanings you identify in the writing. Is the author trying to convey a message?

_____ Complete planned experiences.

_____ Evaluate

Notes

_____

_____

_____

_____

_____

_____

_____

STUDENT RECORD   for _____

Novel _____ Week _____

Discussion Date _____ Pages _____

Questions

_____
_____
_____
_____
_____
_____
_____

Planned Experiences (Skill Activities)

_____
_____
_____
_____
_____
_____
_____
_____
_____
_____
_____

QUESTION RESPONSES

Page	Para.	Ques.#	Key Words	Comments

DISCUSSION EVALUATION

	weak		strong
Member Preparation	0	———	—— 10
Courtesy	0	———	—— 10
Contributions from Everyone	0	———	—— 10
Quality of Responses	0	———	—— 10
Quantity of Responses	0	———	—— 10

Comments: _____

_____

_____

_____

Leader _____

Group Members _____

_____ _____

_____ _____

_____ _____

Date _____

Novel _____

Pages _____

PERSONAL EVALUATION

Rank each item by deciding how well you met the standard. Place a check on the scale somewhere between 0 and 10, weak to strong, to indicate your evaluation.

	weak	strong
Personal Interest	0	10
Preparation for Discussion	0	10
Participation in Discussion	0	10
Vocabulary Activity	0	10
Story Analysis Activity	0	10
Other Experiences	0	10

Comment: _____

_____

_____

_____

_____

_____

My plan for improvement: _____

_____

_____

_____

_____

Knowledge - Recall
Comprehension - Explain
Application - Use
Analysis - Take Apart
Synthesis - Make It New
Evaluation - Judge It

These six levels of thinking represent a hierarchy of skills. They were developed by Benjamin Bloom in the *Taxonomy of Educational Objectives.*

The first three levels represent simpler processes and require little critical thinking. The others are often called the "higher levels" of thinking and are the main thrust in activities presented in this book.

The following section provides activities to help you understand these six levels of thought and to show you how to form questions based on each of the levels. Later you will be able to identify the level at which you are thinking, working, or asked to work.

The activities in the remainder of this book have been keyed to Bloom's Taxonomy in the upper left corner for your convenience.

Bloom's Taxonomy

Have you ever played that game? In this variation your task is simply to compose ten questions about this week's section which can be quickly answered "yes" or "no" by others in your group.

Question	Answer	Page

E

The ten-question task was fairly easy and now you are ready to use your questions on your group. Have a "yes," "no" session during which all members have chances to ask and answer questions. Following the session, write your reaction to this type of activity.

Reaction: _____

_____

_____

Rank the question session on this scale:

		strongly disagree		strongly agree
1.	We learned many new things.	0———————————+——————————10		
2.	We thought deeply and intensely.	0———————————+——————————10		
3.	We felt stimulated and challenged.	0———————————+——————————10		
4.	We showed creativity.	0———————————+——————————10		
5.	We found the task dull and boring.	0———————————+——————————10		
6.	We were asked to recall information.	0———————————+——————————10		

**Your work on questioning was at the
KNOWLEDGE LEVEL
of thinking.**

Forming questions which ask for facts to be recalled is a type of thinking often classified as knowledge. At this level of thought the learner shows in some basic way knowledge of some basics. Questions often start with words such as who, what, when, or where. The learner may be asked to match, list, recall, underline, pick, say, or show.

At the knowledge level it is easy for us to decide whether an answer is correct or incorrect.

Write five knowledge level questions about yourself. Share questions and answers with a friendly partner.

_____

_____

_____

_____

_____

_____

_____

_____

_____

_____

_____

RETELL THE STORY

Get together with your group and spend some time summarizing this section of the book round robin style. The first person begins the story and tells a bit about what happened and then allows the next person to continue, and so on.

In this type of activity you are functioning at the Comprehension Level of thinking, showing that you *understand* what you have read. Questions at this level ask the learner to restate something, rewrite, give an example, illustrate, define, summarize, or otherwise prove that the knowledge or basic facts have become internalized.

Main idea questions are at this comprehension level, as are vocabulary questions which ask you to define or use the word in question as you understand its meaning from the reading.

Get together with your group to help each other form a set of comprehension level questions. First, each member should record two or three questions which are probably at this level. Then questions should be read aloud and a decision made as to whether or not they fit the comprehension mold. After the discussion place "Y" (yes), "P" (probably yes), or "N" (probably no) beside each of your questions. Following the activity write your reaction to this type of questioning.

Questions _____

_____

_____

_____

_____

_____

_____

_____

_____

_____

Reaction _____

_____

_____

_____

APPLICATION

At the Application level you are asked to use your knowledge in some way. The question may ask you to organize your facts, construct some model, draw or paint an example, collect data from the reading, demonstrate, or dramatize an event.

Many times you *apply* your knowledge in reading by preparing a poster, a mobile, a new book jacket, a sculpture, a scrapbook, or some tangible item to share your interpretation of the reading.

Think about ways you could *apply* your understanding of this week's reading section. With your group form a very large chart of Application projects for reading.

From the class list select one application of interest to you and complete it.

Share your project with the class.

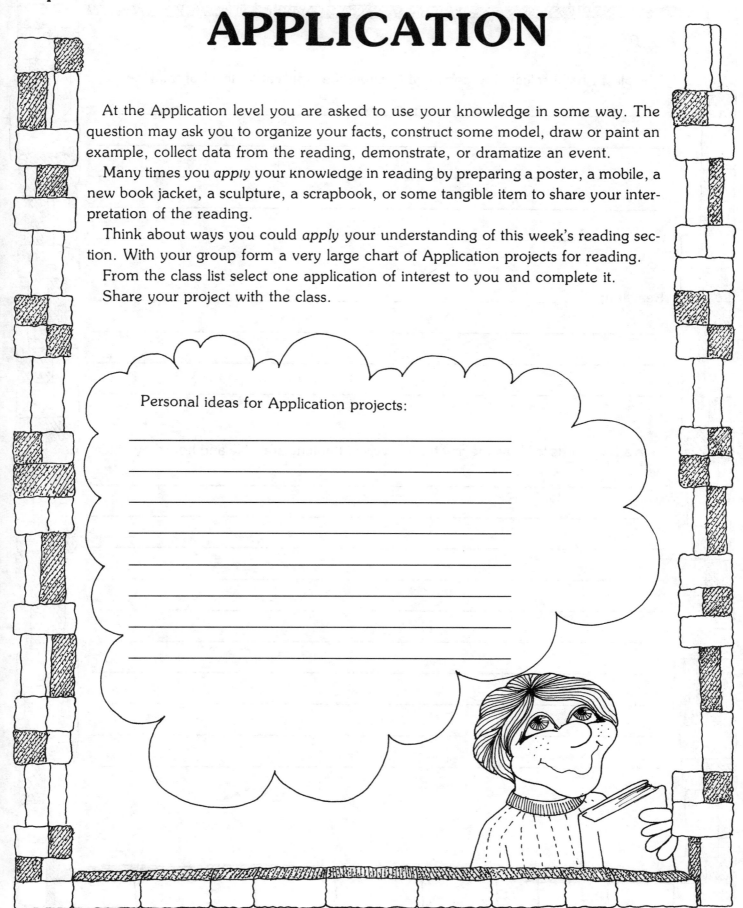

Personal ideas for Application projects:

_____

_____

_____

_____

_____

_____

_____

Ap, E

Project I have selected to complete to show the Application level of thinking:

_____

_____

_____

_____

_____

Reaction: _____

_____

_____

_____

In a few words tell how the first three levels of thinking are alike and how they differ.

_____

_____

_____

_____

_____

_____

_____

_____

_____

_____

_____

ANALYSIS

The Analysis level asks the learner to examine the facts, to classify, survey, experiment, categorize, or explore. The student is to look at something in depth. Most of the reading questions your teacher presents for each section are at the Analysis level.

On the spaces below list some of the problems (major or minor) faced by characters in your book thus far. You won't find these on a page labeled "problems." This task requires you to *examine* and to *classify* what you have read. This is Analysis.

_____

_____

_____

_____

_____

_____

_____

_____

Now look at your list of problems. Can you categorize them in some way?

_____

_____

_____

_____

_____

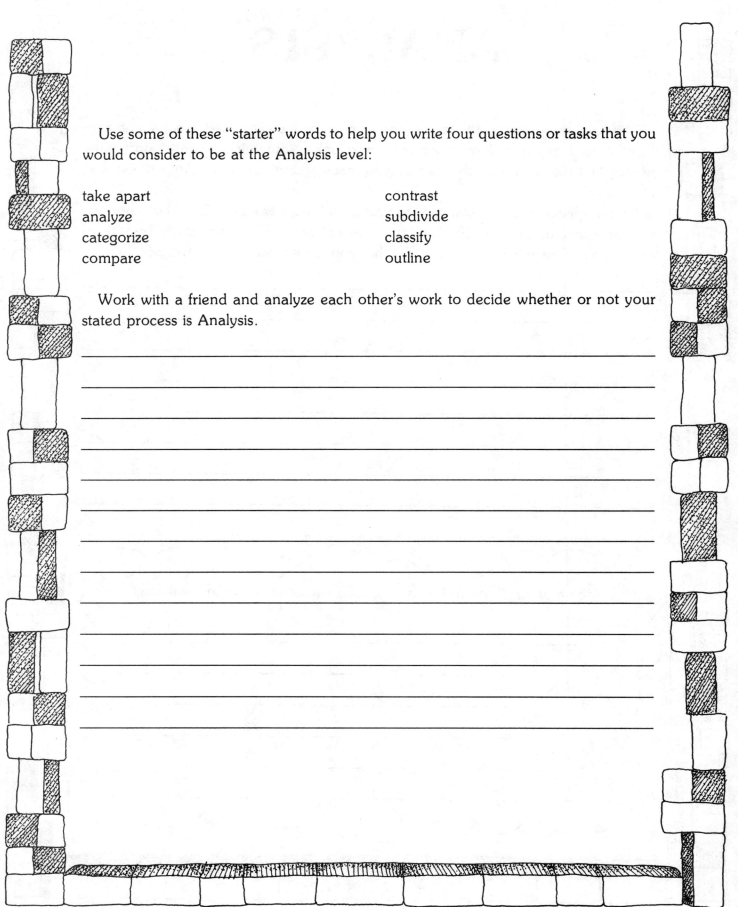

Use some of these "starter" words to help you write four questions or tasks that you would consider to be at the Analysis level:

take apart   contrast
analyze   subdivide
categorize   classify
compare   outline

Work with a friend and analyze each other's work to decide whether or not your stated process is Analysis.

_____

_____

_____

_____

_____

_____

_____

_____

_____

_____

_____

_____

_____

_____

SYNTHESIS

The Synthesis level of thinking is perhaps the most exciting and creative level of thought. It is at this level that your mind plays around with this new information you have read or received and forms new images that can take the form of ideas or inventions. The knowledge you received *combines* with what you already have to make a new connection.

Here are some good process and product words for Synthesis:

Process	Product
imagine	game
combine	invention
role play	show/script
compose	song
invent	story
predict	diagram
create	model
design	product
adapt	cartoon
develop	poem

Mix and match some processes with some products to come up with three Synthesis activities—one for you, one for a book character, one for a special talent your teacher has—all related in some way to your novel.

Ap

SYNTHESIS ACTIVITIES

For me: _____

_____

_____

_____

_____

_____

_____

For character: _____

_____

_____

_____

_____

_____

_____

_____

_____

_____

For my teacher: _____

_____

_____

_____

_____

_____

_____

_____

_____

EVALUATION

Most people think of evaluation in the sense of, "Did I do a good job?" This is certainly one form of evaluation, probably the most familiar. When we consider evaluative thinking, we go beyond wondering about somebody's opinion of us and our performance.

We become thinkers who judge anything or any person *according to some standards* decided upon beforehand. The setting of standards or criteria is very important so that we may have something to compare to the product or idea we hope to judge.

Many activities in this book ask you to rank performance, effort, or feelings on a scale, to criticize a character's feelings or actions, to debate the importance of a particular event, or to comment upon the value of a particular activity in your own learning. These are examples of Evaluation.

Self-evaluation is the best way to determine how well you are learning. Consider what things are important to know or to practice in order to improve your critical reading ability. Brainstorm ideas with your group. List some here.

(Example: understanding word meanings) _____

_____

_____

_____

_____

_____

_____

Ap, E

Select five skills you should definitely possess. Rank your ability in each area in some way.

_____

_____

_____

_____

_____

How will you know if you improve or master the skills you have selected? Think of a way you could evaluate your progress.

_____

_____

_____

_____

_____

_____

Try an image

Get ready for a mind journey . . . relax all your body parts . . . close your eyes . . . and open your mind's eye . . . in front of you place a book . . . make it small, about the size of a peanut . . . who will read it? . . . place a reader in front of the book . . . now make the book and the reader grow larger and larger . . . .

Test out the above mind journey on a friend. Discuss the experience. What can you think of for continuing this image-making story? Will the book reader become larger? angry? disappear? Just about anything can happen as you use your imagination.

Training your mind's eye to see things in different ways helps you to become more flexible in your thinking.

Now think of something that is flexible (a sneaker, a sock, a pancake, a blade of grass) and create a mind journey.

Read it to a friend. Talk about the images formed. How could they get better? Could your writing be improved or would your friend's learning to visualize in a better way be more successful? Both?

A Flexible Journey

Record your mind journey here. _____

_____

_____

_____

_____

_____

_____

_____

_____

_____

_____

_____

_____

_____

_____

_____

Comments about this Flexible Journey: _____

_____

_____

_____

_____

_____

_____

Imagery Sharing

Prepare a mind voyage for your group by selecting a section from your novel to read aloud. As you search for a passage consider one that appeals to as many senses as possible. After you have chosen your reading, try it out with a friend. Have the other person read it aloud to you as you relax and form clear mind pictures. If you are satisfied with your selection, prepare it for reading to the group. You may want to skip parts of it. Be sure to read clearly, distinctly, and slowly enough for group members to get the picture. Try to recall your own mental images as you read it.

My reading selection _____

                                                    pages

Vivid words and phrases are _____

_____

_____

_____

_____

My selection especially appeals to these senses: _____

_____

CRAZY IMAGERY

Record any ten objects. Beside each add an adjective/noun combination found in this week's reading.

Object	and	Adjective and Noun
_____		_____
_____		_____
_____		_____
_____		_____
_____		_____
_____		_____
_____		_____
_____		_____
_____		_____
_____		_____

Think about combining the objects and adjective/noun combinations. Form mind pictures. Make them humorous! Write your three funniest images in sentence form.

_____
_____
_____
_____
_____
_____

Brainstorm a Mind Journey

Have one group member read aloud about ten lines from the novel as the rest of the group close their eyes and concentrate on image making. When the reading is complete have each member jot down three words that come to mind. Collect all the words.

Another group member now slowly reads the words, one at a time as the group tries to imagine new associations in personal mind journeys.

After the experience share some of the images and mind stories that were created.

Wordless Story

Think about ways you could tell a story without words. What can you use? How can you share your mind pictures with someone else without writing or saying any words? List your ideas here.

_____

_____

_____

_____

_____

Choose one of these ways to use on your novel story section. Try to do it. Test it on a friend. Discuss your results and write a comment.

_____

_____

_____

_____

_____

WHAT IF?

Picture these in your mind.

What if all the characters in your book turned into animals? What would each become?

What if someone in the story had a magic nose? Who would it be? What would the nose do?

What would happen if everyone grew to be giant-sized or shrunk?

What if the main character had an imaginary rabbit friend?

What if every green thing turned purple?

What if a war started? How would it change the novel?

GET DRAMATIC

With your group choose a few pages from this week's section that would be suitable for dramatization. Choose a narrator and select character parts. Practice reading with expression. Tape your dramatic reading and play it back for your evaluation.

Your group may decide to act out the selection with gestures, simple costumes and props. Each actor should try to "see" the character being portrayed in his/her mind's eye. Imitate facial expressions and body postures and movements suitable for the particular character.

Perform only after several practice sessions to smooth things out. Judge audience reaction to your presentation.

Be an Illustrator

Most novels leave all the picture making up to your mind's eye, but often a publisher asks for a few sketches to accompany the writing for the book jacket or for advertising purposes.

Think about this week's reading section. Which events or places or people are most vivid in your mind? Try not to think about them in words, only in pictures. Can you see one with all its details?

On a separate paper do some sketching until you are satisfied with one. Keep referring back to your mind's picture as you need help.

Characterization

CHARACTER SILHOUETTE

Choose a character. List adjectives which most nearly fit that person. In the blank silhouette draw or paste pictures which reflect the adjectives you have chosen.

_____

_____

_____

_____

_____

_____

_____

_____

_____

_____

In the space below write a physical description of the character you have selected. Try to limit your writing to exactly thirty-five words.

_____

_____

_____

_____

_____

_____

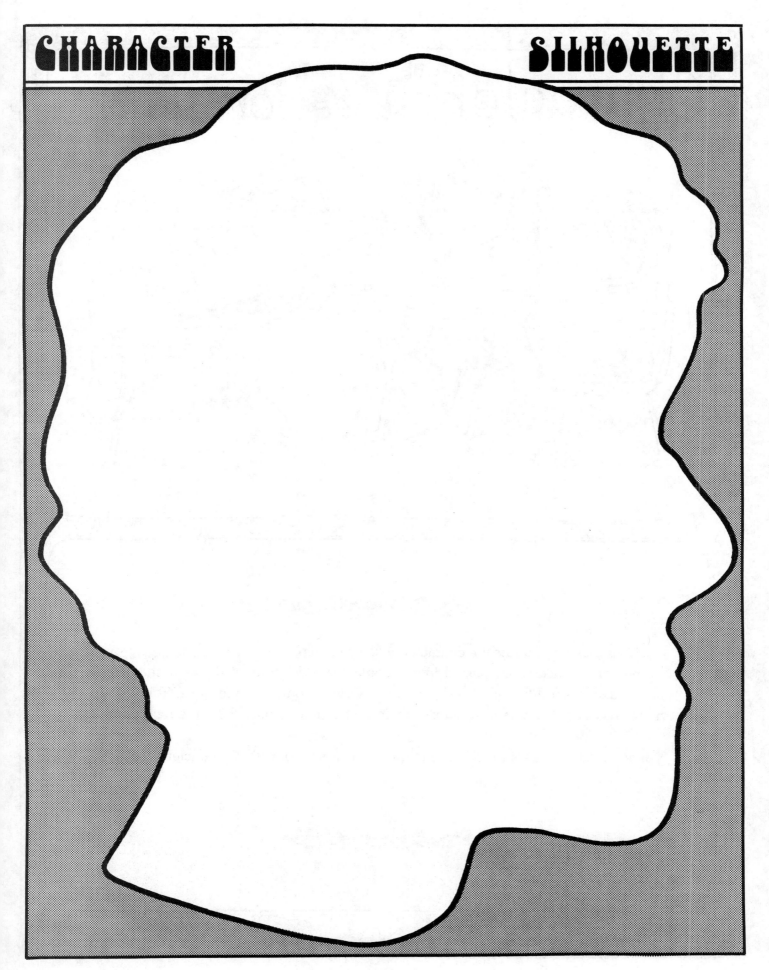

Character "Yes" or "No"

This is a game of guess the character which can be played in a small or large group. Names of characters are placed into a container. One student draws a character's name and responds with "yes" or "no" answers only to questions from group members. The first person to guess the correct character may draw the next name.

Variation: Questioners may ask only questions that deal with a character's feelings.

Character Time Capsule

Think about things that are very important to one or more of the characters. Consider items that would be of lasting significance. Select five things you think the character would have placed in a time capsule to be left for future people to open from a time capsule one hundred years from the time of placement.

Write a couplet (two-line rhyming poem) to accompany each item.

_____

_____

_____

_____

_____

_____

_____

_____

_____

_____

_____

_____

_____

_____

_____

_____

An

CHARACTER QUOTES

Select several characters from your book. From the reading you have already done, choose a quote for each person that seems to say something important, either directly or indirectly. Then locate a famous quotation or saying (try *Bartlett's Familiar Quotations* at the library) which you feel each character would choose as important.

_____

_____

_____

_____

_____

_____

_____

_____

_____

_____

_____

_____

_____

_____

_____

_____

_____

_____

Character Tree

On the following page design a character tree similar to a family tree, but showing the various branches as important people in a central character's life. Perhaps one branch would show family (or would this be your character's root system?); one branch might show work or school friends.

Be very creative and imaginative as you create your tree.

Consider showing special features such as blossoms, fruit, blight, fallen leaves, various seasons, weather, or times of day to symbolize the variety of relationships.

Character Tree
for _____

THEIR FAVORITE THINGS

Choose two characters. Make lists of their favorite things, places, sayings, friends. Note any items they seem to have in common.

What do these lists of things tell about the personalities of each character? Write briefly about each person, describing each in general.

_____

_____

_____

_____

_____

_____

Select a character and create a bagful of possessions for that person. Present it any way you choose . . . words, pictures, dramatic display of real items . . . .

_____ 's Bag

CHARACTER SIMILE

Choose ten descriptions from the Physical and Emotional Adjectives sheets. Select those that would apply to particular characters.

For each word selected, form a sentence that contains a simile about a character. Example: Harry was as fierce as a full-blown tornado.

_____

_____

_____

_____

_____

_____

_____

_____

_____

_____

_____

_____

_____

_____

_____

CINQUAIN A CHARACTER

A cinquain poem has five lines. It has a definite pattern but does not require rhyme.

Line one: one word   Michael
Line two: two words   Gentle giant
Line three: three words   Helping many people
Line four: four words   His courage is unique
Line five: one word   Policeman

Select a book character. Try to capture something special about that character in a cinquain.

_____

_____

_____

_____

_____

_____

_____

Now write a cinquain about yourself.

_____

_____

_____

_____

_____

T-SHIRT

The T-shirt rage reflects a special way for individuals to display a special message or personal idea.

Design a T-shirt picture and slogan just right for one of your novel's characters.

Using fabric crayons, place your completed design onto a T-shirt.

Character Collage

Cut words and pictures from magazines to create a special collage for your favorite character.

INTERESTING INTERVIEWS

To get a profile of one of your novel's characters, work with a partner to improve your interviewing techniques. One of you will assume the character's role and the other will conduct the interview.

The person representing the character should review book passages to prepare for questions on the thoughts, personality, and problems.

The person who will conduct the interview should plan ahead to decide on important areas for discussion. Four or five probing questions should be prepared to serve as a guide for discussion.

During the interview the character may elaborate on an area and give more details than the book offers, but should stay within reasonable bounds for what the character would probably say. A true attempt should be made at really visualizing and assuming the role.

The interviewer should complete note taking in any form that is comfortable. Following the interview, the information gathered should be organized and prepared for presentation. Write up the interview and combine it with others done in the class to compile a magazine similar to *People*. Examine an issue to determine what sections to include.

Students not responsible for recording interviews should assume other roles and responsibilities for the production.

List tasks to be completed and assign jobs. Be sure to choose a magazine deadline.

Task	Responsible Person	Deadline

Issue will appear at your local newsstand on _____.

PHILOSOPHY OF LIFE

Often the reading of a book helps us to sort out our feelings about things. When we have a set of beliefs and values that seem to stay the same, we are beginning to develop a personal philosophy.

Meet with your group to discuss what it means to have a philosophy of life. Seek help from your teacher or library books if you seem to need it.

When you have a good understanding of this idea, choose a book character who seems to have a philosophy similar to your own or who seems to have influenced your personal feelings, either positively or negatively.

On a separate paper record the things you think that character values or believes. Combine your ideas into a well-formed paragraph which will indicate the character's philosophy of life.

Now form another paragraph which reflects *your personal* philosophy of life.

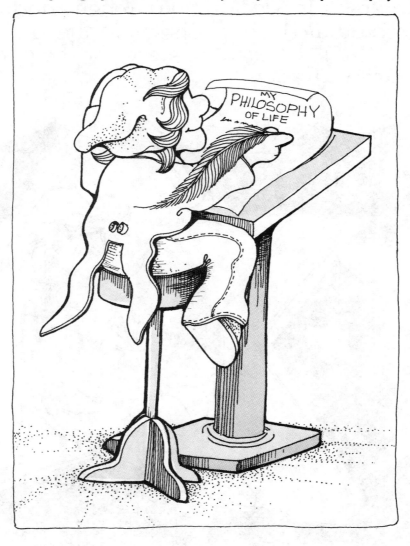

ADD A CHARACTER

Think about a famous person you feel could be smoothly written into your novel in a "cameo" appearance. Be sure the person is of the correct time period.

Find out enough about the famous person to decide how, when, and where you could write him / her into the action. Write about it or write a scene for the person to dramatize.

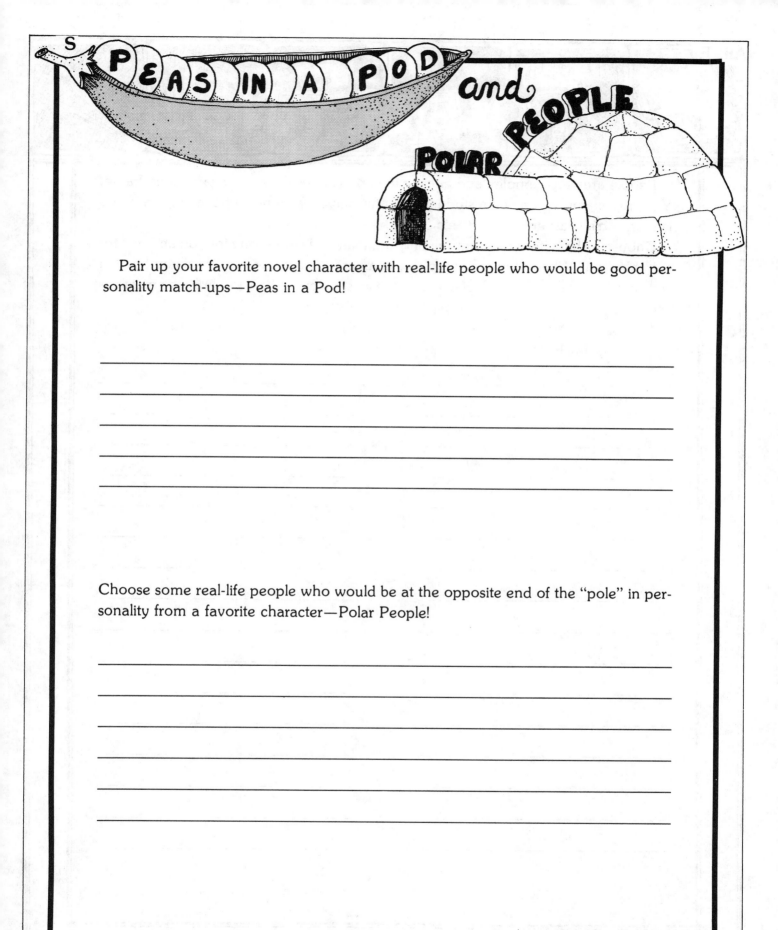

S PEAS IN A POD and POLAR PEOPLE

Pair up your favorite novel character with real-life people who would be good personality match-ups—Peas in a Pod!

_____

_____

_____

_____

_____

Choose some real-life people who would be at the opposite end of the "pole" in personality from a favorite character—Polar People!

_____

_____

_____

_____

_____

_____

ROLE LISTING

People are very complex and engage in various roles during the same time frame. You, for example, may be a student, a tennis player, a friend, a pet owner, a group leader, a dishwasher, an artist, etc.

Choose a character from your reading and make role lists—one for you and one for the character. When they are complete, compare the lists. ✔ any roles you have in common. * the favorite roles of each. = the least favorite roles. Put *D* by the most difficult.

My Roles	's Roles
_____	_____
_____	_____
_____	_____
_____	_____
_____	_____
_____	_____
_____	_____
_____	_____
_____	_____
_____	_____
_____	_____
_____	_____
_____	_____
_____	_____

To the student

The purpose of the activities in this section is to help you become more aware of words and more adept at using particular words you select from your reading.

The words you choose to study do not have to be the most difficult to pronounce or the longest you can find. The best words to choose are those you have seen before but you don't ordinarily use. These words are ones you will probably meet again and it will be to your advantage to learn about them and their variations.

Sometimes you won't be able to find any "new" words for your vocabulary. In this case just select the most interesting ones you can find. As you use them in the vocabulary exercises you are sure to find out something new.

A dictionary should be your friendly companion as you prepare your vocabulary work. An interesting side effect of dictionary work is the "extra" information you pick up along the way to the word you are searching for. Most of us can't resist a peek at some other word or illustration that catches our eye. That's incidental learning. Enjoy!

Vocabulary Precision

PERSONAL WORD FILE

Record vocabulary words on 3" x 5" index cards and file alphabetically in a small file box.

Review words frequently and think of new ways to use your words.

* SUGGESTED ACTIVITIES *

1. Select three words at random. Use them in one sentence. Repeat with other words several times.
2. Choose ten words. Write variant forms of the words. Add endings, prefixes, suffixes.
3. Choose ten words. Discover the origins of these words. Add this information to your cards.
4. Select ten words. Write them in syllables.
5. Create a game using selected words from your file. Be sure that demonstrating an understanding of word meanings is one of the requirements of the game.

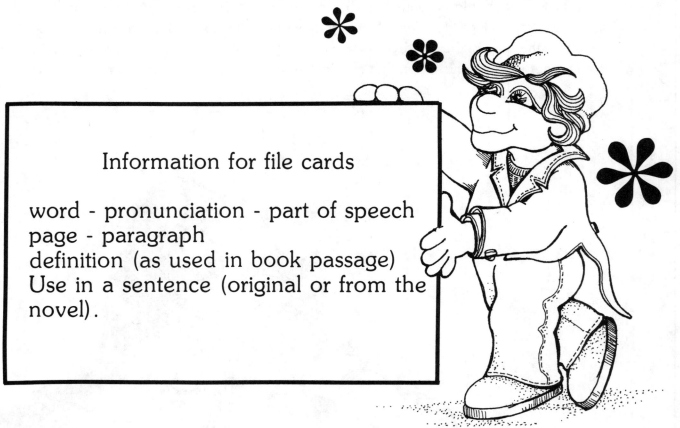

Information for file cards

word - pronunciation - part of speech
page - paragraph
definition (as used in book passage)
Use in a sentence (original or from the novel).

WORD LINKS

Using a list of about ten words from this week's reading section, form word links for each word, showing other thoughts and ideas you associate with each.

Vocabulary words: _____

_____

_____

_____

Word links:

Example:

VOCABULARY CONTEST

The Preparation

Here's a contest anyone can win!

On the chart list your best challenge words from this section's reading. You will be trying to stump other group members with definition challenges.

Page	Para.	Word		Definition (as used in passage)

The Contest

Group members take turns offering words for defining as used in the passage. Person giving correct response scores 1 point. If no one can define the word, the challenger receives 3 points.

Game continues until each member has presented five words. Count up points to determine winner.

Variation: Every member writes a response and can receive points for *every* word presented.

Acrostic Puzzles

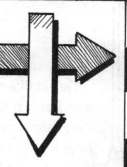

Choose five words from your reading section. Record each word vertically. Now think up other words to "fit" horizontally. Add a word clue for each of these horizontal words. Now you are ready to present your work as a puzzle to a partner. You may decide to leave your original word in the puzzle, or maybe you prefer to leave all letters *except* the original word, or leave all blanks!

Here's an example:

a *mbitious*   eager to work; not lazy

n *octurnal*   occurring in the night

c *reate*   to make something new

i *sland*   body of land surrounded by water

e *vening*   late p.m.

n *orth*   direction

t *eeth*   chewing instruments

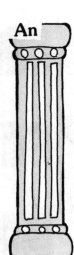
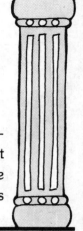

PERSONAL PROPERTIES

Select fifteen words from this week's reading section by closing your eyes and pointing. Record the words. Think about the *properties* of the words themselves or what they symbolize (their color, size, weight, form, texture, function, shape). Then see how many ways you can group (classify) your words. You may use the back of this paper to show your groups.

Word	Properties

Wordcycle

Select ten words from this section's reading. Choose a starting box and record one of the words. Relate that word to another on your list and join the two recording your selected word and the relationship. Continue around the circle.

Do some require a "force" fit? Good! You'll really have to think!

CONNECT A PAIR

Select twelve vocabulary words from your reading. Record them in two columns. Now form six pairs of words and form some connection with each separate pair. Tell how they are alike, or different, use both in the same sentence, make up a new definition for the pair as used together, or create your own pairing activity.

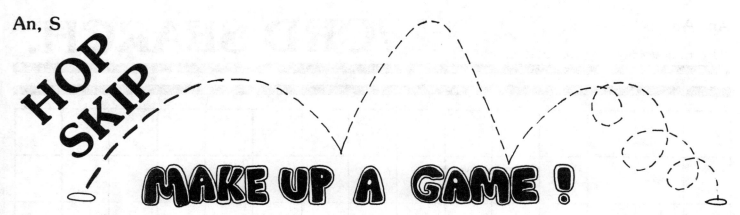

Select twelve words. Record only every other letter and follow each with a synonym or definition.

Challenge a friend to fill in the blanks.

Example: s__ g__ e__ t   a piece or separate fragment of something; portion

answer: segment

_____

_____

_____

_____

_____

_____

_____

_____

_____

_____

_____

_____

_____

Variation: Skip only vowels.

Use new vocabulary words to create a . . . **WORD SEARCH.**

WORD LIST

sensible Words

Locate words or phrases that appeal to the senses. Record below. Can you find all 5 senses?

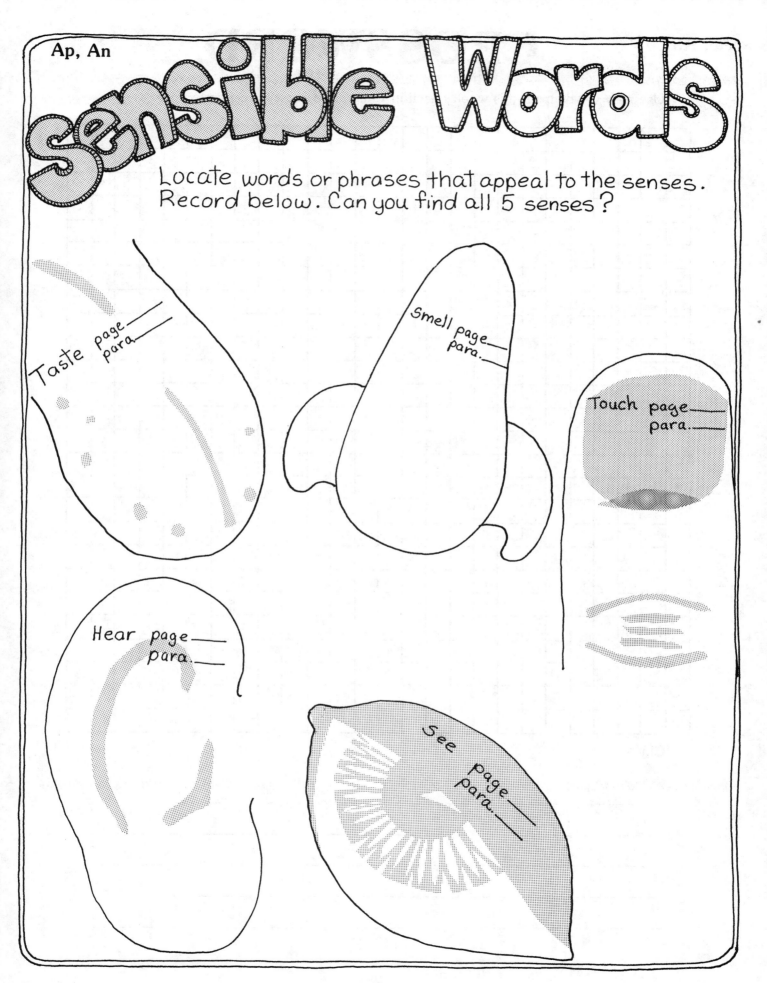

Taste page____ para.____

Smell page____ para.____

Touch page____ para.____

Hear page____ para.____

See page____ para.____

CROSSWORD

Use new words from this week's section to create a crossword puzzle.

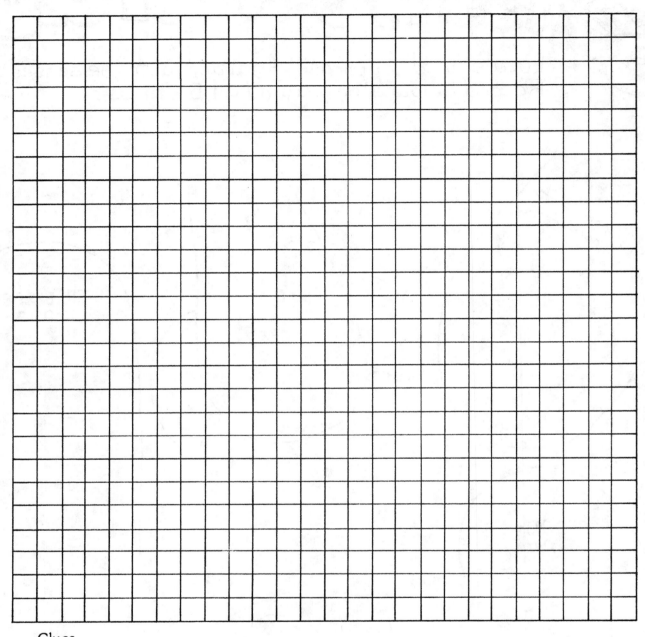

Clues

_____

_____

_____

_____

_____

An

Word Webs

Select ten words to web. Place each word in a center. Web each one by adding lines and words to show synonyms, antonyms, and other word associations your mind can make.

Example:

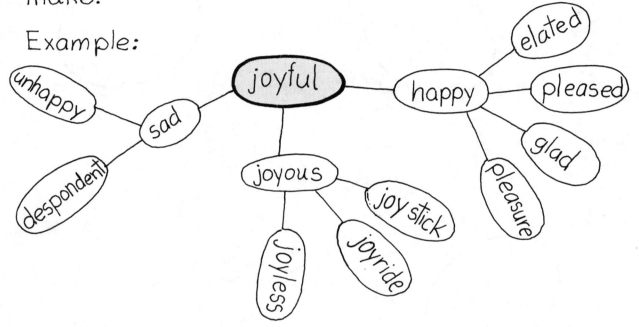

You may choose to use color to show the various parts of your web.

Share your webs with another student. Are there any branches of your webs that you need to explain.

Variation:
Choose a partner and make a game of Word Webs. Fill in everything except your central words. Challenge each other to fill in the centers.

Word Webs

An

CATEGORY

List here twelve words from your reading section.

_____   _____
_____   _____
_____   _____
_____   _____
_____   _____
_____   _____

Think of a way to fit all twelve words into categories you select. Use a variety of categories. Try to be *unique!*

Category	Word Members

*Challenge: With a partner, share lists and try to guess the headings for your words.

FINDING FEELINGS

Record below the feelings shown by characters in this section of the novel.

Page	Para.	Feelings	Characters(s) Involved

Choose five feelings from your list. Record each on a slip of paper and drop them into a container. Each member of your group adds his/her slips to the pile.

Now take turns selecting a "feelings" slip and have a skimming race to see who can locate a book passage to read aloud in which that feeling is stated or implied. The passage does not necessarily have to be the same passage you have recorded.

Extra! Extra! Read All About It!

Locate and clip words from newspapers to form headlines for incidents from your story. Add in writing any extra words you need.

Now write a brief news story. Your editor has limited you to fifty words. Be sure to cover the 5 W's—who, what, when, where, why.

_____

_____

_____

_____

_____

_____

_____

_____

_____

_____

_____

_____

_____

_____

_____

_____

FEELINGS MAP

The creation of a feelings map may help you to see the way one character's emotions influence the feelings of others and their resulting actions. Your map may become very elaborate! The details of the story may cause your map to take interesting twists and turns.

Your first map should focus on only a small section of the novel. When you become more adept at mapping feelings you may want to make separate maps for each section and then intertwine the sections.

Perhaps your whole group would enjoy making a large feelings map together. Be prepared for some disagreements. Individual interpretations will differ.

To begin a feelings map you could start with the information you prepared for a Feelings Identification page.

Here is a simple map to show you the way! Use circles for feelings and diamonds for events.

EPISODE ANALYSIS

Choose some event or happening from your current reading. In a few words write down what happened. Mention events and people involved.

_____

_____

_____

_____

_____

_____

_____

_____

_____

_____

Initiating Event - What was the circumstance that caused this event to happen?
Reaction of Main Character - What did the main character in this episode do? Did this response cause the character to take some course of action?
Consequences - Outcome

Initiating Event	↔	Reaction of Character	↔	Action of Character

Consequences of Action-Outcome

GROUP SEQUENCE

Each group member records two events that happened during the reading from this section. The slips of paper with these events are then placed into a container and drawn out in turn by group members so that each person has two event slips written by someone else.

The group then works together to place all events in their logical sequence according to the story. Duplicates may be placed together. Group members should listen carefully to events as they are read to determine whether the ones they have should come before or after the one being discussed.

START

SECTION PYRAMID

Build a pyramid summary of this section. In the outline place one word for a central character, two words to show important feelings he/she displayed, three words to describe where the main action took place, four words to tell an important event, and five words to tell about a problem that still exists.

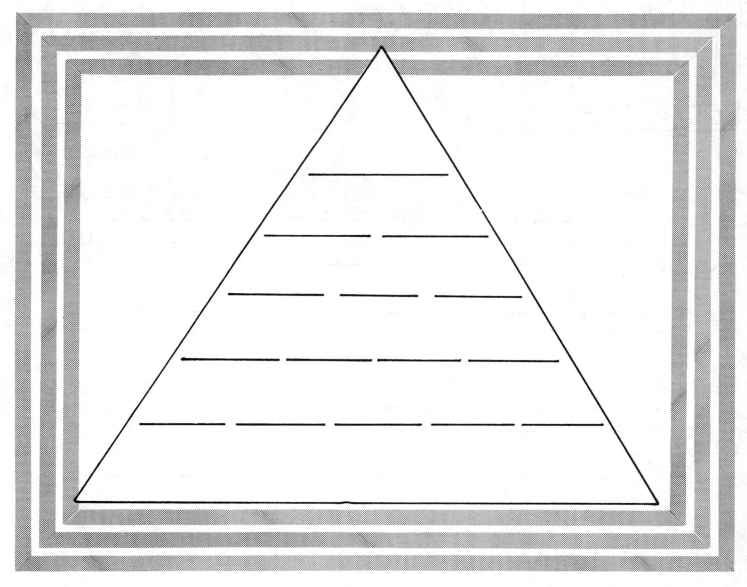

SOLVE A PROBLEM

Understanding how characters solve problems can help you to analyze real-life situations.

Choose a dilemma or problem presented in the section you read.

The problem: _____

_____

Facts: _____

_____

How was the problem solved? _____

_____

_____

_____

_____

What other ideas would you have for solving the same problem?

_____

_____

_____

_____

What do you think is the most practical solution to a problem like this?

_____

_____

_____

_____

_____

_____

CLUES TO TIME

How does the author handle the passage of time in your novel? Find time words or references in the current section of the novel.

_____

_____

_____

_____

_____

_____

_____

_____

Decide on some visual way to show the passage of time in this section of your novel or in the entire book up to this point.

Perhaps you would like to try a time line or show the time passing on a clock face. Maybe you have some other way to show it. Be creative!

OTHER PLACES, OTHER TIMES

Select items from this reading section that would not exist or would definitely be different if the story were set in a different place or time. Think up another place or time and a replacement item for each.

Item	Other Place/Time	Replacement Item

Where Am I?

Think about the places which are described in your novel. Invent a humorous character who will visit these places. Prepare a written mind journey to present to your group. The first part should introduce the new character in detail and the rest of the mind journey should lead you all on an adventure to familiar places from the novel with your new character.

SPECIAL PLACES

What are the special places mentioned in this section of the novel. Can you visualize them? Choose one of the following activities:

1. Design a map with symbols for each important location.

2. Create a sketch or drawing showing one place. Be elaborative and show many details.

3. Show a footstep progression picture naming places a main character visited in the correct sequence.

Example: Mary's footsteps

NAME IT

Authors face a very important decision when selecting a book title. Readers are frequently turned on to a book simply by noting its title.

Think about the novel you are reading and make a list of other possible titles. Star (*) the one that appeals to you the most. Take an informal survey of others who have read your book and place check marks ✔ beside their favorites from your list.

_____

_____

_____

_____

_____

_____

_____

_____

_____

Can you think of an important consideration in selecting a particular book title? This is a criterion or standard a title would have to possess. Write one here.

_____

_____

_____

WHAT'S IN A CHAPTER

Authors have definite reasons for separating their works into chapters. Look over the last three chapters you have read and consider the reasoning behind these chapter divisions.

For each chapter tell why you think it makes sense to end at that particular point. If you disagree with the division, tell why.

HOT AND COLD

If asked our feelings about a particular book, we often haven't stopped long enough to analyze our general reactions. This exercise is designed to help you sort out your emotional responses to one section of your novel.

Step one: For each page of reading, mark a number 1 to 10, weak to strong, to show your *level* of feelings when you read that page.

Step two: Add up all the ratings and find your average feelings rating. Record your average on the feelings meter.

PAGE	COLD									HOT
	1	2	3	4	5	6	7	8	9	10

Step three: Select two pages you gave a "9" or "10" rating and tell what prompted your emotional response.

_____

_____

_____

_____

_____

_____

_____

_____

Creative Explorations

A NOVEL MUSEUM

Future generations would like to remember the happenings from this novel by visiting a museum of artifacts.

Each member of your group should select three to five important items to display. In addition, each member should record three to five important facts.

The entire group should decide where and how the museum display is to be set up. Tour guides should prepare a brief talk to accompany the display.

Date for display: _____

Items to be displayed: _____

_____

_____

_____

_____

_____

_____

Interesting facts:

_____

_____

_____

If a real display is not possible, sketch or create scale drawings of the display.

Be a Friend

When we are faced with a problem, it often helps to get some good advice from a friend. What sort of problem has one of your book characters faced lately? Write a letter to him or her, giving encouragement or advice as you would to a good friend.

An

Saying the same sound at the start of several words in a series is an artful accent that adventuresome authors address as *alliteration*. This special play on sounds in words is a terrific technique for quietly highlighting particular passages in a radiant rhythm. Identify several alliterative passages from your reading and record them below.

Page	Para.	Alliteration

Now create some original phrases or sentences that are alliterative. Have them relate to a character or event from the novel.

_____

_____

_____

_____

LOCATING COMPARISONS

Similes and metaphors are used by authors to help the reader form more vivid mind pictures. Locate several examples from your reading. Remember that similes express comparisons using "like" or "as," while metaphors do not.

Page	Para.	Comparison	Simile or Metaphor

Select a comparison from those you listed that is especially vivid in your mind. Illustrate the comparison on a separate sheet of paper or write in words the mind picture you see.

PROBING QUESTIONS

A good researcher is first of all a probing questioner. Practice in forming interesting questions is time well spent.

If the author of your novel were available, what questions would you want to ask? Prepare a set of questions being sure to cover who, what, when, where, why.

_____

_____

_____

_____

_____

_____

_____

_____

_____

_____

_____

_____

Is it possible to get your questions answered? Do some research on the author to determine the answer. If so, how will you go about it?

SPEED SKIMMING

Work with your group taking turns reading short parts from this week's reading. After the section is read aloud, other group members race to skim material and locate page and paragraph. Give five points to the person who locates the passage first, four points for the second person, and three points for the third. Continue play until everyone has had a chance to read a section. Total up points to determine skimming champ.

LISTING IDEAS FOR FLUENT, FLEXIBLE THINKERS

1. List every character.

2. List ways your novel says "said."

3. List any foods mentioned in the book.

4. List ways the author shows size.

5. Write a problem solved in your novel.
   List other ways it could have been solved.

6. Open your novel to any page. Find the name of an object. Make that your list heading. List uncommon uses for the item.

7. List happy thoughts about your novel.

8. List places mentioned in the novel.

9. List ideas or things you think the author of this novel believes.

10. List the best places to read a novel like this.

MORE CREATIVE EXPLORATIONS

1. Select a passage that makes *you* feel a particular emotion. Locate a work of music that gives you a similar feeling. Reread the passage as you listen to the music in the background. Do you find that the feeling you have grows more intense? Would the music you selected provide a good background for a dramatization of the passage? Test your opinion on a friend to see if you both reach the same conclusions.

2. Make a series of abstract drawings in color to accompany several passages that give *you* strong feelings. Show your drawings to a friend to see if your particular feelings "show" in the pictures.

3. Work with a partner or small group. Take turns reading aloud short passages that make *the reader* feel something. Those listening should express their feelings through facial expressions and body movements (placement, posture, dance, or a combination).

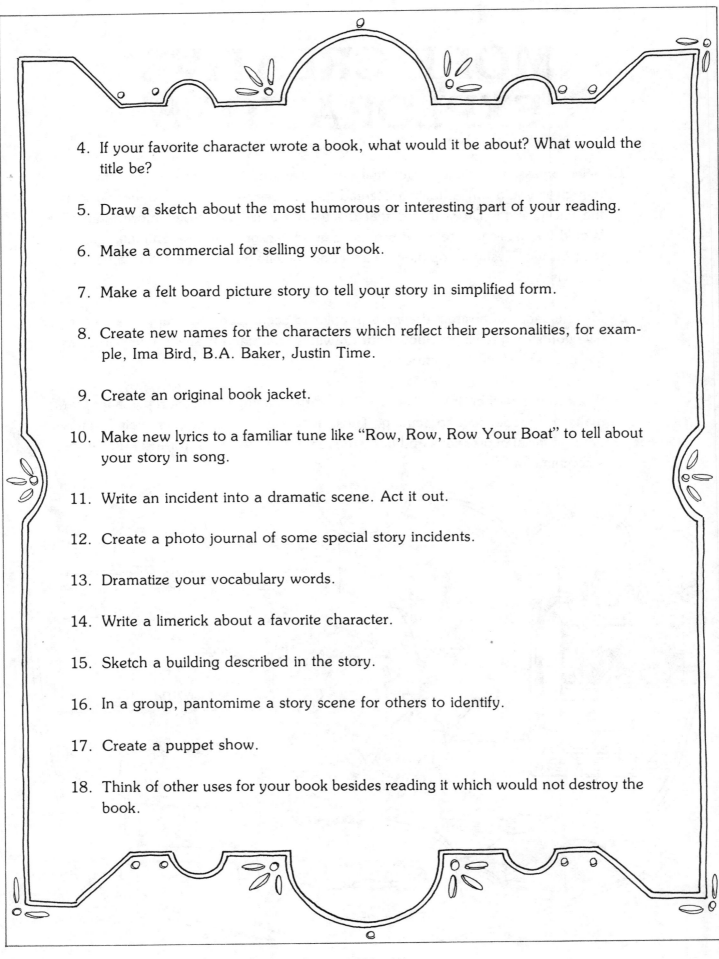

4. If your favorite character wrote a book, what would it be about? What would the title be?

5. Draw a sketch about the most humorous or interesting part of your reading.

6. Make a commercial for selling your book.

7. Make a felt board picture story to tell your story in simplified form.

8. Create new names for the characters which reflect their personalities, for example, Ima Bird, B.A. Baker, Justin Time.

9. Create an original book jacket.

10. Make new lyrics to a familiar tune like "Row, Row, Row Your Boat" to tell about your story in song.

11. Write an incident into a dramatic scene. Act it out.

12. Create a photo journal of some special story incidents.

13. Dramatize your vocabulary words.

14. Write a limerick about a favorite character.

15. Sketch a building described in the story.

16. In a group, pantomime a story scene for others to identify.

17. Create a puppet show.

18. Think of other uses for your book besides reading it which would not destroy the book.